MICKLE MAKES MUCKLE

First published in 2007 by
The Dedalus Press
13 Moyclare Road
Baldoyle
Dublin 13
Ireland

www.**dedaluspress**.com

Copyright © Michael Augustin and Edition Temmen, 2007
Drawings © Michael Augustin, 2007
Translations © Sujata Bhatt, 2007
Afterword © Philip Casey, 2007

ISBN 978 1 904556 71 8 (paperback)
ISBN 978 1 904556 72 5 (hardbound)

All rights reserved.
No part of this publication may be reproduced in any form or by
any means without the prior permission of the publisher.

The moral right of the author has been asserted.

Dedalus Press titles are represented in the UK by
Inpress Books, www.inpressbooks.co.uk,
and in North America by Syracuse University Press, Inc.,
www.syracuseuniversitypress.syr.edu.

Cover drawing by Michael Augustin

The Dedalus Press receives financial assistance from
An Chomhairle Ealaíon / The Arts Council, Ireland

MICKLE MAKES MUCKLE

POEMS, MINI PLAYS & SHORT PROSE

by

Michael Augustin

WITH DRAWINGS BY THE AUTHOR

Translated from the German by
Sujata Bhatt

Afterword by
Philip Casey

DEDALUS PRESS

ACKNOWLEDGEMENTS

Some of these translations and drawings first appeared in the following publications:

Cyphers (Ireland); *PN Review, Brindin Press Online* (UK); *Carapace* (South Africa); *Buku Panduan Festival Puisi Internasional Indonesia 2002, Horison* (Indonesia); *Amastra-N-Gallar* (Galicia / Spain); *The Harrisburg Review, Sirena, Glossen* (USA); *The Malahat Review* (Canada); *Odes to the Future—offered to Pearse Hutchinson*, edited by Eiléan Ní Chuilleanáin, A Festschrift, Dublin 1997; *Light Years—A Broadsheet to Celebrate Pearse Hutchinson's 80th Birthday*, Dublin 2007. *Zeitwanderer— Catalogue of Artwork by Ria Eing with Poems by Sujata Bhatt & Michael Augustin*, Cuxhaven 1999. *Flash Fiction Forward—80 Very Short Stories*, edited by James Thomas & Robert Shapard, W.W. Norton & Company, New York 2006. *Prometeo— memorias XV Festival Internacional de Poesía de Medellín*, Medellín, Colombia 2005. A fair selection of translations and some of the drawings (now rearranged in this volume) originally appeared in a bilingual chapbook entitled *Michael Augustin: Gedichte lesen keine Gedichte / Poems don't read poems*, translated by Sujata Bhatt and published by the Max Kade Center, Dickinson College, Carlisle, Pennsylvania, USA 2003.

*for Jenny Mira Swantje
born on St. Brigid's Day*

Contents

SOME QUESTIONS REGARDING POEMS
Some Questions Regarding Poems   11

WHAT IS GOOD TO KNOW
What is Good to Know   19
I Feel Sorry   26
Local Call Lübeck   31
Encounter   32
The Boot Stretcher   33
Umbrella   34
Landscape of Concrete   35
Not to be Forgotten   36
Move On   37
Obituary   38
Burial at Sea   39
Suburbia, around 7:00 pm   40
Philip Glass: Solo Piano   41
Sad Walk   42

NINETEEN FIFTY-THREE
Nineteen Fifty-Three   45
About Poems   54
About Readers   56

NO HAIKU, SAY HAIKU POLICE
No Haiku, Say Haiku Police   61

ASSORTED SHORT CUTS
Assorted Short Cuts   75

PAVEMENT CAFÉ
The Gentlemen Jakobs and Schröder   91
Mrs. Filske   92
Mr. Lehmensieck   93
Mrs. Sebald and Mr. Johnsen   94
The Handbag   95
A Mid-Atlantic Incident   96

In a Pavement Café	97
Opportunity	98

ALPHABET SOUP

Alphabet Soup	101
Out There	102
Horse, Trojan	103
Napoleon	104
Already a Bit Rancid	105
Spectacles	106
Writing	107
House	108
The Writer in a Cage	109
This Story	110
Vita ex Aqua	111
Beauty	112
Early	113
A Writer's Life	114
The Chinese Guy	115
Dog	116
Mirrors	117
Reading	118
Giraffes	119
An Error	120
Birds	121
Love	122
Grass	123
On the Train	124
Burnt Out	125
One Night	126
While Reading	127

CURTAINS

The European Cup	131
Having a Talk	133
Intercity	134
Peace Mission	136

Afterword by Philip Casey	137
Translator's Note	139
About the Poet / About the Translator	140

SOME QUESTIONS REGARDING POEMS

Some Questions Regarding Poems

for Pearse Hutchinson & Martin Mooij

Can poets change the world?
—Gottfried Benn

Is poetry
a continent
or is it more like an ocean?

Are there more written
or more unwritten poems?

How much does it cost
to produce
a poem?

Which poem
says more about its author:
his first one or his last?

How many poems per month
does an average
family of four need
to make ends meet?

Should a poem contain
everything
that is found in the newspaper
or everything
that is not found in the newspaper?

Which words
have never ever
appeared
in a poem?

If one places
a book of poems
on the scales
and it shows 300 grams,
does that indicate
the weight of the paper
or that of the poems?

What is
the opposite
of a poem?

Do poems tend
to be loud
or to be quiet?

How many old poems
fit in a new one?
And how many new poems
fit in an old one?

What is the difference
between a poem with a title
and a poem without a title,
discounting the fact
that one has a title
and the other has none?

Where does one find
the "best before date"
on a poem?

Is it possible
to extend the durability
of a poem
before its time runs out?

Can poems
bring the dead back to life?

Does a poem
have more or fewer lives
than a cat,
and how many lives
does a poem about cats have?

Can one get oneself
vaccinated
against poems?

What in the world
will poems lead us to?

What possibilities are there
to completely forget
a poem
that one had to learn by heart?

How can poems
defend themselves
against being caged
inside anthologies?

What requirements
does a poem have to meet
in order to become
a favourite poem?

Can poems about flowers
multiply
by self-pollination
or do they always need
a poem about bees?

Does a love poem
have to be good in bed?

Which love poems
are better:
the pre-coital
or the post-coital ones?

Are love poems
bound to one person
or are they transferable?

When, at the very latest,
must a short poem stop
if it doesn't want to risk
being mistaken
for a long poem?

Can poems
be produced artificially?

How many poems
can one read, at most,
if one still has to drive?

How can poems
be prevented?

Can a poem sense it
if it's brushed
by the mantle
of literary history?

Should poems
be provided
with the foot-note
"please delete what does not apply"?

May poems
refuse to give evidence?

Should one throw poems
to the drowning?

What do memorable poems
remember?

Do political poems
represent
the interests
of apolitical poems?

How good must a poem be
in order to be forbidden?

Do poems evaporate
if one leaves the book
lying open for too long?

Is earth
the only planet
where poems
are to be found?

Should poems
be deployed
in areas of crisis?

Has the supply
of poems
for the population
been secured?

In case of emergency
are there any reserves of poems
and for how long
would they last?

How long
can a human being
survive
without poems?

WHAT IS GOOD TO KNOW

What is Good to Know

*for Sujata Bhatt, who set me on the trail
with her poem, "What is Worth Knowing?"*

It is good to know
that every twelve seconds
somewhere in the world
a poem is being written
but that only every one hundred and thirty minutes
one is being read.

It is good to know
where the whiskey stands
and where the bottle
with the aspirin,
where the switch is for ON
and where it is for OFF.

It is good to know
that people
who are up to their necks
in deep water,
still have a choice:
between drowning
and dying of thirst.

It is good to know
that, in America, the usual
warning printed on paper cups
stating that the coffee
contained within is extremely hot
apparently also applies
when the coffee contained within
has long gone cold.
(Yes, that's how literature is!)

It is good to know
that one word too much
can be just as appropriate
as one word too little,
but that both words together
are totally wrong.

As the Germans say,
it is good to know
that one always
meets twice
(if at all).

It is good to know
that God
sees everything
but, most of the time, quickly looks away,

that one egg is just like another

and Berlin remains Berlin.

It is good to know
that Frankfurt am Main
actually was supposed to be
completely torn down;
however, already, all by itself
it has become so run down
that there's nothing more
left to be done.

It is good to know
that still water runs deep,
that Art is long
and that life is short
and that statistics lie,
according to statistics.

It is good to know
that pushing up daisies
is very different
from picking them on a sunny day

and that it's not tasteless
to argue about taste!

It is good to know
that Karl Marx and Friedrich Engels
during their daily discussions
in Hampstead
paced up and down the room
continuously following the same paths
so that with the passage of time
and the constant pressure
of the heels of their boots
at the four corners where they turned
small indentations developed on the floor
to the great joy of numerous children
who played marbles at times over there.

It is good to know
that he who doesn't search for anything
is able to find everything,

that the destiny of a bus stop
lies in the fact
that it must always wait for the next bus

and that in view
of the countless minorities
the few majorities
are clearly in the minority.

It is good to know
that what we call
bad weather
is actually good weather
(and that, according to the forecast,
on Thursday the good weather will stop
finally, and at long last.)

It is good to know
that one swallow
does not make a summer
but that a bird in the hand
is worth two in the bush.

It is good to know
that everything we say
can be used against us
but also everything we don't say

and that there's nothing sweet
about being the salt of the earth.

It is good to know
that the Russian writer
Velimir Chlebnikov
warned us not only of three-legged horses
but also of three-legged humans—

alas, to no avail.

It is good to know
that a single pencil
contains
up to thirty thousand poems.

It is good to know
that some writers
are of the opinion
that even a sheet of paper
on which they haven't written a thing
contains more literature
than the complete oeuvre
of all their colleagues.

It is good to know
that a certain
Philos Blake in New Haven,
after being forced to spend
several days
in the company
of well-sealed wine bottles—
out of sheer frustration,
invented the cork screw.

It is good to know
that a single past
can prevent
hundreds,
yes, thousands of futures.

It is good to know
that, because of his
erection problems,
an impotent gentleman
who could no longer see
any other way
than to walk
stark naked
into a snow-drift
was found dead
after days of searching.
With his member frozen stiff.

It is good to know
that love
is a passing condition
between two entities
consisting of
more than 70% water

and that the occasional tear
might flow.

It is good to know
that the apple of temptation,
although causing a great deal of harm,
was chemically untreated.

It is good to know
that the opposite
of the opposite
is the opposite.

It is good to know
that once a year
on the day of the dead
the Romans
sacrificed
a fish with its mouth sewn up
to the Goddess of silence.

It is good to know
that all roads
not only lead to Rome
but also lead away from it.

It is good to know
that not only cribs and coffins
can be made
out of a tree
but also rocking chairs.

It is good to know
that almost one third of Germany
is covered by forest.
Still.

It is good to know
that appetite
comes with eating.

And that too many cooks
spoil the broth.

It is good to know
that everything stays as it is.
(Subject to alterations.)

It is good to know
that people who know
everything they don't know
know everything.

I Feel Sorry

I feel sorry
for the man in the red jacket
who has been longing for a blue jacket
for the past twenty years
but each time buys himself a new red one instead.

I feel sorry
for the winter
that will never live to see the summer.

I feel sorry
for the little children
in whom adulthood
already lurks.

I feel sorry
for the words *in vain*
because they will always remain in vain.

I feel sorry
for the radio signal
filling gaps between programmes
which is put on the air
only so that everyone can hear
there's nothing to be heard.

I feel sorry
for the question
whose answer everybody—and I mean everybody
claims to know.

I feel sorry
for the dungeon
that has to hold out
down there for centuries
without even having been convicted.

I feel sorry
for the barber's apprentice
who of all things
has to accidentally
cut the throat
of his boss's best customer.

I feel sorry
for the preacher
who just can't remember
the word AMEN
and so is doomed to continue talking
until judgement day.

I feel sorry
for the pursuer of happiness
who without knowing it
has long since found happiness
and doesn't have the slightest clue
that it has even started to run out.

I feel sorry
for the echo
that for once
would love to have the first word.

I feel sorry
for the punch line
that always hangs on the end.

I feel sorry
for the second mitten
of the one-armed man.

I feel sorry
for the hamster
in the wheel,

for the goldfish
in the bowl

and for the man
in the barrel—

I feel sorry
for the pig in the cold cut.

I feel sorry
for the serious situation
which everybody mistakes
for a game.

I feel sorry
for the fashion
which happens to be nothing
but a passing fashion.

I feel sorry
for the future
that with every passing second
shrinks
only to add to the size of the past.

I feel sorry
for Berlin.

I feel sorry
for the bathroom mirror
that clearly shows its horror
when I look into it
in the morning.

I feel sorry
for the limits
that will always
have to remain within limits.

I feel sorry
for the pea
on which the princess tosses and turns.

I feel sorry
for the legs
that go all the way up
but then can't go a step further.

I feel sorry
for the first one
who goes over board
and for the last one
who misses the boat.

I feel sorry
for the woman who runs the gallery—
for whom every single *vernissage*
turns into a *finissage* right away.

I feel sorry
for the window
through which everyone looks in
but no one looks out.

I feel sorry
for the dead writers
because they always
have to fill in
for the living.

I feel sorry
for the stare
that goes into emptiness

and for the free kick
that misses the goal.

I feel sorry
for the ascetic
whose pillows
are filled with lead.

I feel sorry
for the parallel lines
because there's no way
to prevent their collision in infinity.

I feel sorry
for Tom Sawyer
who never had the joy
of having children
with his blood brother Huckleberry Finn.

I feel sorry
for this poem.

Local Call Lübeck

Last night
Thomas Mann rings.

Now what does he want,
I wonder,
just can't
keep quiet,
the dead.

But he had only
dialled the wrong number.

Encounter

A little boy
throws a stone
after the soldiers.

They shoot back
and continue walking.

Who, for God's sake,
will follow now
in their footsteps?

The Boot Stretcher

And the boot, that was stretched by the stretcher?
What happened to it?
Well, it lies at Auerstedt,
on the battlefield, that's where it lies,
at Auerstedt.

And the leg, which was stuck in the boot,
that was stretched by the stretcher,
where is that leg?
Still stuck in the boot
that lies on the battlefield at Auerstedt,
that's where it's stuck, the leg.

And where is the man
whose leg is still stuck in the boot
that the stretcher stretched
and which lies on the battlefield now
at Auerstedt?

He's under the earth where the turnips grow,
close by.
That's where he got stuck, the man!

(And he has only one boot on.)

Umbrella

for Adrian Mitchell

When it's grey
outside
my blue one
makes me
a beautiful
sky.

Landscape of Concrete

It's becoming
increasingly difficult
to bury
one's head
in the sand.

Not to be Forgotten

A knot
in the handkerchief

a string
around the finger

a note
pinned on the wall:

We must always
remember
to water
the forget-me-nots.

Move On

In the middle of rush hour
a poem
has occurred:

The police are there right away
and block everything off.

Keep on going,
snarls a cop,
move on.

He puts
prose back in place.

Obituary

Jonas
died
of fish poisoning.

Burial at Sea

A gust of wind
knocks the boat over.
The entire congregation of mourners
drowns.

Only the urn
floats.

Suburbia, around 7:00 pm

The couples
bolt the doors
of their detached houses.

Outside
in the dusky evening
divorce lawyers lurk.

Philip Glass: Solo Piano

for Pearse Hutchinson

This is the music
you want
as you enter the tunnel

This is the music
you need
while you're in the tunnel

This is the music
you hope for
at the end of the tunnel

Sad Walk

for Bob Zieff

Blowing ahead
of me already
the dust
to which I
wore them out
the soles
of my shoes

NINETEEN FIFTY-THREE

Nineteen Fifty-Three

*"The year of my birth – what did the papers say back then –
how did things look?"*
—Gottfried Benn, '1886'

The year of my birth—how did things look?
What was broadcast on the radio?
Which pictures were shown on the newsreel?
Who watched television already? And who looked away?
What was sold,
or who, and to whom?

In 1953, foreign countries
are still foreign countries,
and at the local grocer's
the domestic potato
has the say,
at the butcher's, the sausage.

In 1953,
there is still
a bit more future
than today.

In 1953,
hundreds of thousands
of children and teenagers
are absent from school—
innocently unexcused,
because during the war,
which has ended just eight years ago,
either the grown-ups
have killed them off,
or, owing to the circumstances,

never even fathered them,
let alone gave birth to them.

In 1953, among
the German prisoners of war
still held captive
in the Soviet Union,
the number of flea bites
supercedes by far
the number of twinges of conscience.

In 1953,
one hundred garrulous women
are matched by no less
than 72.5 dumb-struck men.

The per capita consumption
of washing detergents
rises to nine kilograms,
the term "women folk"
is being deleted
from the penal code,
and the Kaiserslautern football team
wins the German championships.

When, in 1953,
equal rights for women
pass into law,
it happens,
typically enough,
on the first of April.

In 1953,
a baker in the town of Rendsburg
succeeds in baking bread rolls
exclusively out of meal worms.

The 760,000 West Germans,
born alive in the year 1953
are welcomed by 28,499 dentists,
who keep their fingers crossed
for careers rich in caries.

While attempting
to introduce in Germany
the tradition
of driving on the left
in Autumn '53,
in Hamburg,
three English soldiers die,
who are, however,
so drunk
that later they cannot
remember anything about this.

Despite the fact
that the government of the GDR
declares 1953
to be the Karl-Marx-Year,
it actually turns into
the year of the writers
whose last name begins with the letter B:

Brecht, Benn, Böll,
Beckett, Bachmann, Borges.

(Apart from that, Stalin dies
and spoils everything.)

Most radio reporters
in the year 1953
happen to be
former war correspondents,
whose words slip out
as if they had still been hatched
in machine gun nests.

To the great cheers of the public,
in 1953,
championships
in running backwards take place.

After years of not having
enough to eat,
in 1953, finally,
German parents
find occasion again,
to forbid their children,
on pain of punishment,
to speak with their mouths full.

In 1953,
against all reason,
England receives
a new queen,
whose fellow countryman Winston Churchill
receives the Nobel Prize for literature.

In 1953,
Paula Rego completes
a painting entitled "1953"—
and Larry Rivers paints his friend,
Kenneth Koch.

In 1953,
for the first time ever,
an international match
of the German football team
is shown live and in full on television.

Although, this game
against Austria ends in a 0:0 tie
and there are few scenes worth watching,
all 1,524 owners of television sets
have gathered in front of their screens,
because there have been rumours
that right after the end of the match
Fritz Walter plans to kick
some of Adi Dasslers hand-sewn footballs
directly into the living-rooms of the spectators,
which, however, doesn't work out even once,
for the captain's very first attempt
shatters the only camera.

The invincible
Emil Zatopek
is determined
to run through the year 1953
in a new record time
of 250 days.

In 1953,
for the first time,
scientists prove clearly
that there is a direct link between
the consumption of tobacco and lung cancer,
whereupon the sales of cigarettes
really do skyrocket,
as if everyone
wanted to smoke a last one
before their imminent demise.

In 1953, when Hemingway
is awarded the Pulitzer Prize
for "The Old Man and the Sea",
old Thomas Mann,
after decades,
manages to return to the sea of his childhood,
and to visit his beloved Travemünde again.

(However, since he has forgotten
his swimming trunks in exile, in Switzerland,
two years later,
he comes back once again with them
and a few days later he is made
an honorary citizen of his hometown of Lübeck.)

1953, once again,
turns out to be a year
in which life's not easy at the bottom:
for every German
trainee and apprentice,
there's an average supply
of 84 slaps in the face,
49 knocks on the head,
and 8.5 kicks in the arse.

In April,
the German chancellor Konrad Adenauer
visits the USA and meets the president,
whom he immediately assures
that no one has the intention
to erect a wall—
whereupon Eisenhower suggests
that instead, at least,
an iron curtain should be put up,
which then promptly happens.

In 1953, the first man
lands on the moon—
however, already during his return trip,
he ends up so irretrievably in oblivion,
that, only now,
in this text
(which means completely unobserved)
he finds his way back to earth.

In 1953,
some old Nazis
celebrate their resurrection,
without really
ever having been
buried in the first place.

In June, 1953,
insurgent workers in Berlin
manage to lay the foundation
for the drama,
"The Plebeians Rehearse the Uprising"
by Günter Grass,
which he will actually write
only years later.

In 1953,
workdays
go like hot cakes
and the Sundays, even more so.

In 1953, it is claimed
that Adolf Hitler works as a baker in Buenos Aires,
setting his sights low on small bread rolls—
for the time being.

During the course of the year 1953,
Welsh poet Dylan Thomas loses
the manuscript of his play "Under Milk Wood"
three times over.
Later, he claims
that giraffes have sexual intercourse
while running at a speed of 80 m.p.h,
and in November he drowns in the whiskies of Manhattan.

In the small Dutch town
of Capelle a/d Ijssel,
in December, 1953,
an under-aged,
desperate orphan
gives birth
to a completely dressed,
well-situated, affluent gentleman,
equipped with a hat, a walking stick and an overcoat,
who in a truly noble gesture
adopts the child right away.

In 1953,
cleverly thought-out illusion machines
are being installed in all cities
with more than 80,000 inhabitants.
Since then, these machines function completely faultlessly,
fooling all inhabitants into believing
that absolutely nowhere and never,
and especially not in cities
with more than 80,000 inhabitants,
have illusion machines ever been installed.

In 1953 everyone
is talking about a deaf mute
who is fluent in twenty-six body languages
and writes poems in five of them.

While television chef Clemens Wilmenrod
still fiddles with an old German dish
of puffballs and chanterelles,
atomic mushrooms flourish
in the desert of Nevada,
and Edmund Hillary
mounts his Sherpa.

In 1953,
the double helix is discovered,
while a certain Godot,
anticipated for the first time
the very same year,
doesn't surface,
and still hasn't surfaced,
even today.

1953 is a year
that one could see
a long time coming.

1953 is a year
which hasn't happened any other time,
before or after.
(And in that respect, it is
similar to all other years.)

1953 is, in the first place,
the year between
1952 and 1954.

In 1953, once again,
one is a little bit smarter
but still not smart enough.

1953 cannot be undone anymore.

About Poems

Poems
are not written,
poems
happen.

Poems
were there
before there were poets.

Poems
are scratched
window panes.

Poems
are decomposable
and therefore must not
under any circumstance
be burnt.

Poems
are open around the clock
(even the hermetic ones).

Poems
from foreign countries
do not require
a visa.
A good translator will do.

No one
should be forced
to read a poem
or even to write one.

Poems
cannot be held responsible
for their author.

Poems
don't read poems.

Poems
can be exchanged
for other poems
at any time.

About Readers

'Writers are always on duty' – Borges

Readers need to have everything in writing.

Readers have a screw loose
in their bookshelf.

Readers read only
what is written out for them.

Readers always see the world
in black and white.

Readers overlook
precisely what they should look at
when reading.

Readers are only after one thing.

Readers let themselves
be lured away
by authors who are total strangers.

Readers happily agree
to be chained to the page;
they follow the order of words,
they are Peeping Toms.

Readers pay
to be insulted by writers.

Readers would like to,
but they can't.

When readers are drunk
they read everything double.
When they are sober
they read only half.

Readers couldn't care less
what they read:
a poem by Gottfried Benn
or the small print
on the tube of toothpaste.

Readers should read
each others' minds,
they should read
between the washing lines
or they should read
their tea leaves
but they shouldn't read books!

Readers actually do believe
that every single word
was written just for them.

Readers don't realize
that there's a difference
between the words
'machine gun'
and 'chewing gum'.

If readers could read
they would read
something else.

NO HAIKU, SAY HAIKU POLICE

NO HAIKU, SAY HAIKU POLICE

You're no haiku! Say
haiku-police. I am what
I am, says haiku.

Far out at sea
the poet in his pedal boat:
Watch it, you icebergs!

*

Bestselling author
takes a walk in the forest.
Stop him—save the trees!

*

As for the plums
in the fridge: I did not eat them.
The old poet did.

Risen too early
I look back jealously at
my snoring pillow.

*

The short night
has taken nine months:
Baby's cry awakens us.

*

How our little girl
chases the butterfly.
No, how it chases her.

The scare-crow chases
a shoal of flying fish back
into the ocean.

    *

The two towers are
gone forever—but the hawks
still fly around them.

    *

The old hairdresser.
The broken pair of scissors.
The hair growing on.

The mushroom pushes
up a cobblestone to let
the earth take a breath.

*

The little word 'love'.
Look out whose mouth it comes from.
But do kiss me first.

*

A guilty conscience:
the lawn-mower has cut off
the violet's head.

In the coffin rings
the phone: Easter is coming.
Time to rise from death!

*

Tulip with no scent.
The girl sprinkles a little
rose water on it.

*

Do not paint the egg.
Do paint the hen. Make Easter
a movable feast.

The watch-dog goes mad.
Little moped buzzes by.
Evening smokes grass.

*

Sun setting in the
rear view mirror—the driver
turns his headlights on.

*

Without that cloud's help
the sinking sun would surely
have drowned in the sea.

The end of summer sale
is cancelled: this summer's end
is not for sale!

*

Ice on the pavement
with a strong taste of chocolate:
the little child cries.

*

Steaming hot meadows.
August. A snow plough rotting.
We laugh while it lasts.

Warm voice of the dead:
*Please leave message on machine.
I will ring you back.*

*

The murderer pulls
it out and shows us the way
with the bloody knife.

*

The dead dog's echo
keeps on barking angrily
but it does not bite.

Like poisoned Snow White
in her coffin: tiny fly
displayed in amber.

*

Because it got stuck
in the branches, the sun has
to shine all night long.

*

Sitting lazily
on the sofa, he tells his
shoes to take a walk.

Along the cross-bar
a nightcap of last week's snow.
Shot off post. Blizzard!

*

One more drink before we go.
And yes: No ice, please!
Winter waits outside.

*

When it's getting dark
and no one looks at him
the mask of evil smiles.

Just missed a haiku
at the haiku-stop—will have
to take the next one.

ASSORTED SHORT CUTS

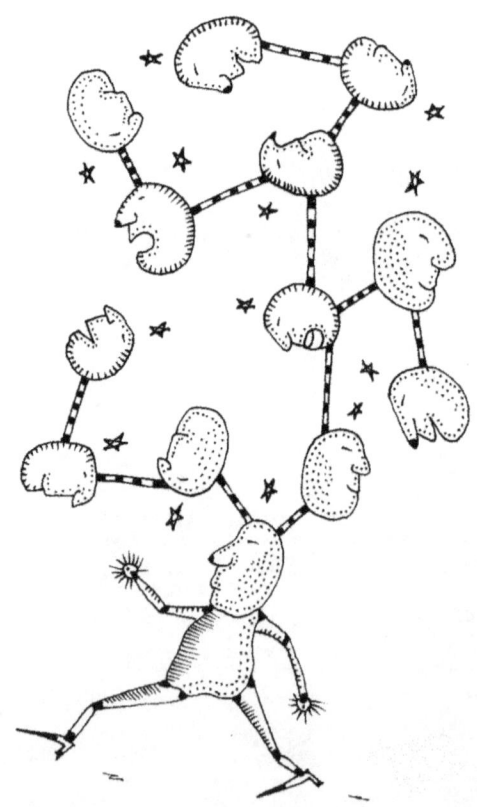

There are productions
of *Romeo and Juliet*
in which
owing to budget cuts
the parts of the lovers
had to be deleted

*

For a bespectacled person
the entire world
lies behind glass

*

Chameleons
at all times
have the original colour
of chameleons

The bagpipe
has the voice of the animal
whose skin has been peeled off
to make it

*

The earth is the heaven
into which the dead
actually enter

*

In eternity
everything
takes that bit longer

In order to cut costs
from now on
two mezzo sopranos
will be replaced
by just one full soprano

*

Elephants must die
so that tiny elephants
can be carved
out of their tusks

*

Colour as such
has no colour

The flea
in the kangaroo's fur
leaps the highest

*

Greatness
is swollen
pettiness

*

The stench
is the howl
of transience

If you pour the contents
of a half full
and a half empty glass together
then you'll have one glass
that is completely empty
and one that is completely full

*

Our skin
is the garbage bag
of our soul

*

Mountainous landscapes
consist of
stacked up valleys

Hedgehogs
feed on
barbed wire

*

In the holes
of the cheese
there's a constant
smell of cheese

*

Among murderers
the murderer of the king
is king

A notorious liar
who lies so much
that in the end
no one believes
he's lying

*

Our long-term memory
is patched together
out of a series
of short-term memories

*

A book
obviously written entirely
by using the space bar

The light
at the end of the tunnel
is the headlight
of the oncoming train

*

For the blood-drenched knife
of the murderer
all help arrives too late

*

Mothers
are the founding fathers
of mankind

Even on the tiniest
common denominator
there's always space
for two

*

Ears would also
like to make noise
sometimes

*

The life
of a smoker
is measured
in cigarette-lengths

The weather
never changes
it always remains
the weather

*

Colourful things
throw
colourful shadows

*

Pigs
are people
without deodorant

Dust
is powdered water

*

Shoes
use people
to get ahead

*

Sleeping cars
snore

The shadow
cast by the lantern
is fully convinced
that it's he
who casts the lantern

*

Just before sunset
even small people
cast long shadows

*

Stairs cannot
make up their minds
whether they lead
up or down

Empty appointment calendars
are filled
with forgotten dates

*

The clock
is a device
which enables us
to turn time
forward or backward
as we please

*

Transience
is the only thing
that will truly
last for ever

Whenever one thinks
that the future
is beginning

it has already
taken another step

ahead

**

PAVEMENT CAFÉ

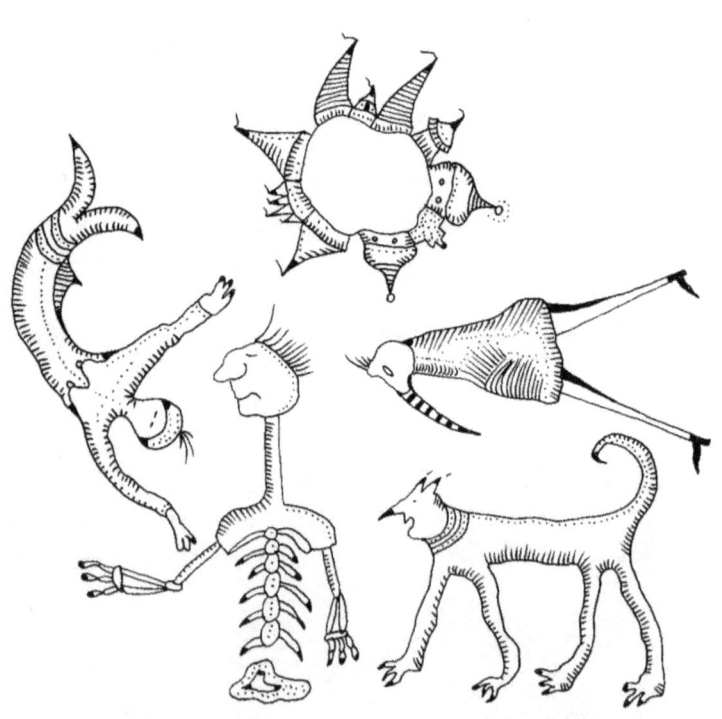

The Gentlemen Jakobs and Schröder

Mr. Jakobs and Mr. Schröder have just been discharged. Mr. Jakobs from the State Prison, Mr. Schröder from the State Hospital. Both go for a couple of pints.

Mr. Schröder, who has just been discharged from hospital, punches Mr. Jakobs, who has just been discharged from prison, right in the face; whereupon Mr. Jakobs is taken to hospital and Mr. Schröder to prison.

Mrs. Filske

Since Mrs. Filske had almost always been oppressed by her spouse, she decided to poison him, which turned out to be a great success, and for a moment brought upon her the feeling of the most wonderful freedom.

But when it came to dismembering the corpse, which happened to be dreadful, backbreaking work, she had to confess that she just missed him terribly.

Mr. Lehmensieck

Mr. Lehmensieck was born into an old Hanseatic family of boozers. The father drank like a flatfish, the mother like a boom bird, which the boy found simply atrocious.

One fine rainy day, he threw his schoolbag into the river Weser and went to America for forty-six years. The parents were beginning to get worried. However, when he returned in the forty-seventh year, he also drank like a sponge, and the two old ones could take their boy proudly into their arms.

Mrs. Sebald and Mr. Johnsen

While Mrs. Sebald and Mr. Johnsen are walking hand in hand in broad daylight, an enormous hole opens up, barely 300 metres further to the left, into which fall: a long-distance runner, two bicyclists, as well as a bus, filled with passengers to the very last seat.

The neighbours naturally talk about it for weeks. Mrs. Sebald and Mr. Johnsen! And the two of them hand in hand! Can you imagine that!

The Handbag

A certain Blunk, who has made a name for himself as a professional thief of handbags, finds himself, on the occasion of one of his assaults, confronted with eighty-two-year-old Elisabeth Schröder, whose handbag he intends to snatch by applying the usual quick, powerful, jerking motion.

Now, what frequently happens in this situation is that elderly ladies, out of sheer fright, forget to release their grip, and thus are pulled to the ground, whereupon they invariably acquire a fracture of the upper part of a thigh bone before they finally let go of the strap and the robber, who runs away.

Completely different, however, is the case with eighty-two-year-old Elisabeth Schröder. It doesn't even occur to her to let go of the handbag. Therefore, as a consequence, Blunk is compelled to drag the old lady behind him, through the bushes, diagonally across the extensive lawns of the park, yes, through the entire inner city, straight into a commuter bus and right out again, for hours on end, until Blunk, who is really quite a strong and athletic young man, can barely continue due to exhaustion, and so finally has to come to a standstill, right in the middle of the street.

This, of course, is the moment that eighty-two-year-old Elisabeth Schröder has just been waiting for. In a jiffy, she bounces back to her feet, and now it's her turn to drag the horrified Blunk behind her for so long until she can't anymore and then it's his turn again.

This has been going on for three years now and everyone thinks that there's something sweet cooking between the pair of them.

A Mid-Atlantic Incident

Two long-distance swimmers, completely independently of each other, set out to cross the Atlantic, one of them from America to Europe, the other from Europe to America, without the usual publicity hassle and without the seemingly unavoidable accompanying life-boats.

Late one night, the weather was mild, the sea was calm, and it just so happened that both swimmers, who had by then reached the latitude of the Azores, crashed head-on with such magnitude that for a little while they entirely lost their sense of orientation.

After swimming around each other in small circles, in a total daze, and heroically withstanding this painful interruption, they decided to continue their watery journey, firmly believing in their ability to reach the goal they had each set for themselves.

Inconceivable was their disappointment, when each of them, at their journey's end, immediately after setting foot on the supposed other continent, had to realize that they had—obviously as a consequence of their oceanic collision and the ensuing short-term loss of orientation—actually swam on in the direction opposite to that which was originally intended, and thus—instead of reaching the scheduled destination—had returned to their respective starting-points.

It has been reported, that both swimmers, out of sheer desperation, have, completely independently of each other, drowned themselves the very same day.

In a Pavement Café

The fat lady who walks by with a little dog, stands still all of a sudden, pulls a gun out of her handbag and shoots twice into the air. Then, she takes the frightened animal on her arm and scuttles away. "She did that on purpose!" says the waiter. "Otherwise the dachshund would never have allowed her to have him on her arm." "But she was really having him on, ha, ha!" I say jokingly. "You're right," says the waiter, "and lucky! Because sometimes she forgets to shoot into the air, and simply fires straight ahead. Last week, for example, she accidentally shot a young man who sat there exactly where you are sitting now." "Oh," I say, "then these are not wine stains on the tablecloth?" "Hell no!" says the waiter as he walks away, "that's blood!" At that moment, I see the fat lady just turning around the corner again. Next to her trots the dachshund. "The bill," I call out, "but please hurry!"

Opportunity

An actor, who was offered the chance of a lifetime to play the part of a glass of beer gave everything to fulfilling this role by remaining as true to nature as possible, which meant for example that he, who had been addicted to drink for decades, immediately renounced alcohol for this purpose. Unfortunately however, and one must formulate it so, the actor was able to deliver such a perfect, realistic enactment, a flawless embodiment of beer, that just a few minutes before the premiere, while the curtain was still down, a thirsty stagehand drank him up in one gulp.

ALPHABET SOUP

Alphabet Soup

Before I started school, I used to love alphabet soup. Precisely and only because the initial letters of my first and last names were swimming in there. The rest of the alphabet consisted of meaningless noodles.

Out There

Out there in open Nature with soaking wet shoes. The cuckoo lets himself be heard. "Cuckoo," he calls, "cuckoo!" The only bird who knows his name, I think, and don't realise how wrong I am. "Magpie", screeches the magpie, "magpie!" And doesn't even stop. "Lark, lark, lark!" A trilling from above. "Blackbird, blackbird!" The blackbird joins in. "Sparrow, sparrow, sparrow, sparrow!" sputters out of the underbrush. "Common curlew, common curlew, common curlew!" I cover my ears and listen deep within myself. "Cuckoo," it says, "cuckoo!"

Horse, Trojan

A Trojan horse has been installed in the inner city, which understandably causes a certain amount of unease among those classically-educated inhabitants, who prowl around the horse deep into the night, prepared, of course, for the worst. Once, however, it emerges that the horse is empty, everyone goes home, relieved, and that which we call 'general emptiness' today can spread itself out fully.

Napoleon

Long before Napoleon, it is said that there were people who claimed to be Napoleon.

Already a Bit Rancid

There are things in life which one, as a mature human being who has already become a bit rancid, should leave to the young without any qualms. Ageing, for example.

Spectacles

In the dead writer's house, his thirty-six pairs of spectacles are displayed. He couldn't see properly through any of them. But even he didn't know that, the man who is still famous, till this very day, for all the breadth of his vision.

Writing

Writing doesn't mean, of course, that one puts new words on paper. The challenge is to cross out as much as possible of the horrible mass of existing words, so that something remains to be seen between the lines.

House

A house, which except for a cellar that contains nothing, contains nothing.

The Writer in a Cage

After his capture, the American writer was kept in a cage. There he sat for weeks on end, and watched the birds flying over the fields in circles. After months, when the door of his cage was finally opened, the writer simply flew away.

This Story

for Jorge Sagastume

"We'll take this story," says the editor, "it's pleasantly short. We must, of course, leave out the beginning, as well as the end."
"But then there's nothing more left of it!" I exclaim horrified.
"That's precisely why we're taking it," says the editor.

Vita ex Aqua

LIFE COMES FROM WATER, so it is written in large letters on the building where the fish shop is. Try telling that to someone who has drowned!

Beauty

In order to observe beauty, each time he had to put on his ugly pair of spectacles.

Early

There's a man who gets out of bed early every morning, and who goes to bed early every evening. Morning after morning, and evening after evening: out of bed, into bed, out of bed, into bed! He's been doing this for the past four and a half decades. One wonders, what will ever become of him!

A Writer's Life

Got stuck in a poem as a boy. Never got out of it for the rest of his life.

The Chinese Guy

A guy from China, who is known as 'the Chinese guy' to all the inhabitants of the little town of Stockelsdorf, returns to his native land one day, due to homesickness, where he is quickly absorbed amidst his 1.3 billion fellow countrymen, and disappears forever. Only in Stockelsdorf, does everyone still know, to this very day, exactly who is meant when someone says, 'that Chinese guy'.

Dog

This supposedly selfless little dog, who for weeks, yes, even for months, holds out by the grave of his master and doesn't even feel like touching his bowl of food: a shrewd beast, cold-bloodedly seeking nothing but his own advantage, a hypocritical mutt who simply knows exactly where the best bones are hidden.

Mirrors

Breathtaking, those moments in which a mirror, without any prior announcement, reveals pictures from its past: Goethe at Frauenplan in Weimar, sticking out his fever-white tongue at us; a totally plastered and jolly Thomas Jefferson at his plantation in Monticello just after he successfully tested his wine-delivering dumbwaiter, a contraption invented and constructed by himself; or my grandfather from Lübeck as a young buck, half an hour before he encounters my mother's mother; not to mention myself, this morning at seven when everything was still different.

Reading

One time the poet had to deal with a particularly malicious audience. Instead of the usual procedure of the audience simply sitting quietly and listening attentively to his lyrical recitation, it was he who was forced to sit for two hours, as if nailed to his ridiculous chair, and listen to the people reciting their own poems.

Giraffes

The day will come, his doctors had warned him, when you'll be able to stand up straight only by hanging on to two giraffes. And don't believe for a moment that they will be there for you. The day did indeed arrive: but contrary to every doctor's prognosis, two of those shy creatures from the African savannas immediately hurried over to his side and promptly offered their assistance.

An Error

Shortly after seven in the morning, the entire rush hour traffic is called back. On the way to work I hear it on the car radio. "An error has occurred!" says the announcer, "please return to your homes immediately and start again from the beginning".

Birds

It has been noticed recently that every day there's a moment when, as if by prearranged appointment, birds all over the world break off for a short while whatever contact they might have with the ground and lift themselves up in the air—all at the same time. As if, in view of some kind of immanent doom, they wanted to assure themselves of their advantage, yes, even their superiority.

Love

When the woman he loved above all, but who despised him, gave him a short, sharp punch in the face, he immediately collapsed head-first into the snow, writing a breathtakingly beautiful love poem with his bleeding nose.

Grass

This moment, when the freshly-cut grass stops smelling of freshly-cut grass, and the chopped blades have long been busy with nothing other than growing back with all their might in anticipation of the next lawn-mower.

On the Train

Accompanied by two gentlemen initially unknown to me, I enter the compartment in the couchette with its three fold-up berths. It soon becomes clear that one of the gentlemen is exactly ten years older than me, while the other one is ten years younger. Since I am definitely older than one of them but at the same time younger than the other, it follows that I am the only one who embodies the entire tragedy of the generation gap, and therefore both of them let me have first choice of the berths. Thus, we travel forth, on rumbling bunks. Next morning, in Zürich, all of us feel we have grown ten years older. But then again, what difference does that make?

Burnt Out

An appallingly bedraggled, burnt-out writer who no longer knows how to help himself except by copying his imitators.

One Night

One night, in a dream there appeared to him, one after the other, all his girlfriends and women. Finally, the whole lot of them ran after him in great anger—attempting to hunt him down. But he quickly hid himself inside his mother.

While Reading

Not without a certain astonishment, I hold the book in my hands. Because every word I read, entire sentences and chapters, disappear as soon as my eyes have grasped them. I turn back two pages and look upon white paper. I leaf forward and continue with my reading. Like an eraser, my gaze slides over the pages, like a Hoover, and approaches the end of the story. At the last moment I shut my eyes tight. So at least the end remains.

CURTAINS

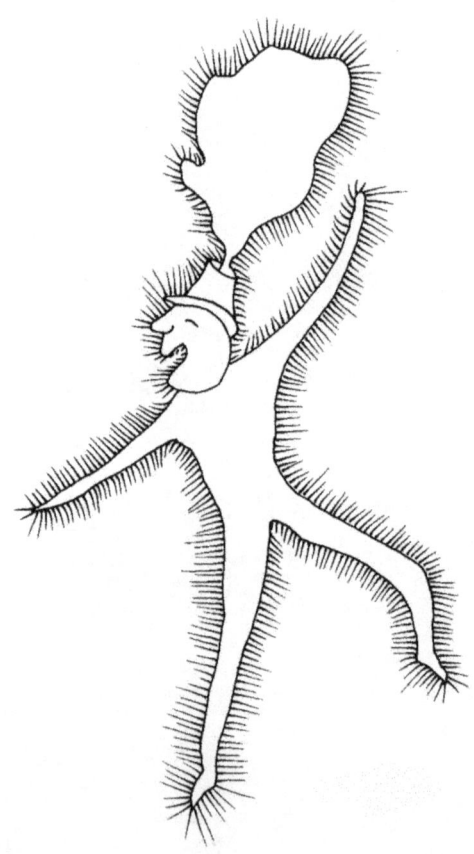

The European Cup

A serious play

Time: 1989, 9:31p.m.
Place: Madrid

The stage is set as a football stadium. Two professional teams, one clad in red and black and the other in green and white, take turns at kicking the ball. A variety of wonderful goals are being scored. In the 76th minute, the centre-forward of the team in green and white falls to the ground.

CENTRE-FORWARD *lies on the ground, writhing with pain.* Mother! Mother!

The mother appears. The referee stops play.

MOTHER   My boy! My poor boy!

CENTRE-FORWARD   Mother!

MOTHER   Who knocked you over?

CENTRE-FORWARD *points at number 5 of the team in red and black* That one there! It was him!

MOTHER   *to number 5*   You should be ashamed of yourself.

NUMBER 5   But it's not true! Your son just fell on purpose.

MOTHER   My son would never do anything like that.

THE REFEREE   Oh yes, yes! I saw it too. He just fell on purpose.

MOTHER   This is none of your business, you snot-face.

THE REFEREE   Now wait a minute! I am the referee.

MOTHER   And you're another loudmouth. Just wait and see. *She gives him a thundering slap in the face.*

THE REFEREE   *writhing on the ground:*   Mother! Mother!

The referee's mother appears.

THE REFEREE'S MOTHER   You're coming home right now! *To the mother of the centre-forward of the green and white team.* And I'll talk to you later!

Exit both mothers with their sons. The match continues. However, owing to the lack of a referee, it degenerates into a deplorable brawl. By and by, all the mothers of all the players appear, as well as the mothers of the two linesmen, the coaches, the physical therapists, the managers, and those of the approximately 30,000 spectators, and take their sons home. So that instead of a final whistle and a final score, there is only a final

CURTAIN

Having a Talk

A Conversation Piece

Time: As stated
Place: A living room

A young married couple enters and, without a word, sits down on the sofa. Several decades pass. Suddenly the husband unexpectedly turns towards the wife

MAN Are you aware, at all, that you really get on my nerves with your continuous silence?

WOMAN *utterly startled* But I haven't even said anything!

CURTAIN

Intercity

A Speedy One-Act Play

Time: 20 minutes late
Place: Between Basel and Frankfurt

Two gentlemen are sitting in a train compartment. The younger one is deeply absorbed in reading a book. The older one looks out of the window

THE OLDER ONE   If you only knew what you are missing!

THE YOUNGER ONE   *feeling disturbed*   What do you mean?

THE OLDER ONE   All that you are missing! If you only knew!

THE YOUNGER ONE   I'm reading.

THE OLDER ONE   Exactly! And at the same time you miss out on reality.

THE YOUNGER ONE   Nonsense!

THE OLDER ONE   *provocatively*   What's there in your book that's so great, hey?

THE YOUNGER ONE   It's the story of two people, a young and an old man, who are sitting in a train compartment. While the young man reads a book, the older one looks out of the window and suddenly claims that his fellow traveler is missing out on reality, whereupon the younger one concisely summarizes the contents of the book and the old one, enraged, calls out: You take me for a fool!

THE OLDER ONE *enraged* You take me for a fool!

THE YOUNGER ONE *unperturbed* Wait a minute, wait a minute—then it's written here, that before the young man can finally return to his book, all of a sudden a curtain falls...

All of a sudden the

CURTAIN *falls*

Peace Mission

A Play of our Times

Time: Late evening
Place: A bedroom

A married couple already lying down in bed has just gotten into a huge argument for the umpteenth time. Outrageously sharp and hurtful words, as well as wet, tear-soaked, heavy pillows, fly to and fro. As the situation for both parties appears to be truly hopeless, the bedroom door is pushed open with a powerful swing, and in storms a young man in full battle gear, recognisable by his blue helmet as a United Nations peacekeeping soldier. Immediately grasping the danger of the situation, he performs a daredevil dive and ends up lying down right in the middle of the bed. The wife to his right, the husband to his left.

BLUE HELMET *out of breath* Refrain from any further skirmishes immediately! Or do you want me to make use of my firearm?

MARRIED COUPLE *Seeking cover under their respective blankets.* No, please don't!

BLUE HELMET Well then, good night.

MARRIED COUPLE Good night.

When both husband and wife have fallen asleep, the soldier gets up without a sound, tiptoes out of the bed, and pulls the

CURTAIN

Afterword
by Philip Casey

A Few Thoughts on *Mickle Makes Muckle*

t

>Does a love poem
>have to be good in bed?

An excellent question, and one of almost fifty searching, amusing and sometimes hilarious questions about poetry and life which surface in the first poem alone.

Now that you've read *Mickle Makes Muckle,* I trust you are in enthusiastic agreement that, along with being funny and quirky, it is intriguing, provoking and ultimately moving. Perhaps also, like me, you're still marveling that these poems were not written in English, such is the quality of Sujata Bhatt's seamless translation.

But what I hope you agree most about is the quotability of so many lines, or rather observations, where assumption after cliché is turned on its head. I first read this book on a computer screen (yes, I know...) and couldn't resist the impulse to copy and paste great chunks of it. I could well be the very man who has longed for a blue jacket these twenty years but each time buys a red one (actually the other way around).

And yes, I really do feel sorry

>for the words *in vain*
>because they will always remain in vain,'

though I still haven't figured out why the poet is sorry for that great city, Berlin.

Michael Augustin and Sujata Bhatt are husband and wife, and world literature is at ease in their household, where poetry in languages such as German, English, Spanish, and Gujarati are taken for granted. There is even a smattering of Irish, such is the familiarity with Ireland, and indeed this familiarity has formed Michael's English-speaking accent, which, on the phone, sounds uncannily like that of the late and lamented Michael Hartnett!

So it is appropriate that Michael's first publication in Ireland included translations into Irish (*Ad Infinitum, Poems and Epigrams,* a German/ Irish/English Selected, translated by Hans-Christian Oeser and Gabriel Rosenstock, Baile Átha Cliath, Coiscéim, 2001).

It's no surprise then, that his association with Ireland stretches back into the early seventies, when he was a student at UCD, and a discoverer of poets such as Pearse Hutchinson, Macdara Woods and Eiléan Ní Chuilleanáin. He didn't just stick his nose in books—he went out into pubs where breathing poets were found (at least in those days), and encountered the real, living thing, and has been doing so ever since. He has earned his dues, so to speak. In these pages he has quoted Borges' remark that 'Writers are always on duty', which is true, and particularly true of Michael Augustin.

All of this adds up to a deep satisfaction on my part—and I know on the part of others, too—that Dedalus has published *Mickle Makes Muckle.*

I trust you agree.

Translator's Note

It has been an unusual experience for me as a translator, working with poems and short prose pieces that I have literally lived with for so many years. Indeed, I have often witnessed the creation of these texts and have been the first listener and reader while they were still a work in progress. Frequently, my comments influenced the further development of respective pieces, which for me at the same time are so rooted in the German language that I am still mystified by the process through which they came to lead a life in English. The author makes extensive use of wordplay, proverbial twists and puns that pose quite a challenge for any translator. Many a time, I have sat in the audience when Michael performed, and even for the umpteenth time it was delightful to be carried away and to join in with everyone's laughter. Knowing his writing makes me smile at the common prejudice that Germans have no sense of humour. May you as readers enjoy Michael's work as much as I do.

Sujata Bhatt,
Conil de la Frontera, 2007

ABOUT THE POET

Michael Augustin was born in Lübeck, Germany, in 1953. He studied Anglo-Irish Literature and Folklore at University College Dublin and the University of Kiel. While still a student he was doing freelance work for RTE and German radio. He now lives in Bremen with his wife, the Indian poet Sujata Bhatt, and their daughter Jenny. He works as a writer and broadcaster with Radio Bremen, where he hosts a fortnightly poetry programme and is the editor for the weekly radio documentary. An author of many volumes of poetry, mini drama and short prose, he has also published several audio books. His poems and drawings have appeared in literary magazines around the globe. Translations of his books have appeared in Argentina, Poland, Ireland, England, Italy and Greece. He himself has also worked as a translator of poetry and drama (Kenneth Koch, Adrian Mitchell, Pearse Hutchinson, John B. Keane, Peter Sheridan, Adrian Henri, Roger McGough, Raymond Carver, Sujata Bhatt, Simon Gray and Matthew Sweeney). He has read at numerous international literature festivals (Dublin, Maastricht, Vienna, Medellín, Caracas, Kuala Lumpur and Makassar) and is the recipient of the Friedrich-Hebbel-Prize and the Kurt-Magnus-Prize. In 1984 he was a member of the International Writing Program at the University of Iowa. In 2003/04 he was Max Kade Writer in Residence and Visiting Professor at Dickinson College in Pennsylvania, and in 2006 he was Writer in Residence at the University of Bath in England.

ABOUT THE TRANSLATOR

Sujata Bhatt was born in Ahmedabad, India in 1956. She grew up in Pune (India) and in the United States. She received her MFA from the Writers' Workshop at the University of Iowa, and now lives in Germany. She is the recipient of numerous awards including the Commonwealth Poetry Prize and the Cholmondeley Award. To date, she has published seven collections of poems with Carcanet Press. She has translated

Gujarati poetry into English for the *Penguin Anthology of Contemporary Indian Women's Poetry,* and has also translated poems by Günter Grass and Günter Kunert. She has been a 'Lansdowne Visiting Writer' at the University of Victoria, in BC, Canada, and a Visiting Fellow at Dickinson College in Pennsylvania. More recently, she was Poet in Residence at The Poetry Archive in London, (www.poetryarchive.org) where more information about her can be found. Her work has been widely anthologised, broadcast on radio and television, and has been translated into more than twenty languages. She is a frequent guest at literary festivals throughout the world.

www.ingramcontent.com/pod-product-compliance
Lightning Source LLC
Chambersburg PA
CBHW022136080426
42734CB00006B/384